"SEA"
INSPIRATION

TO:

FROM:

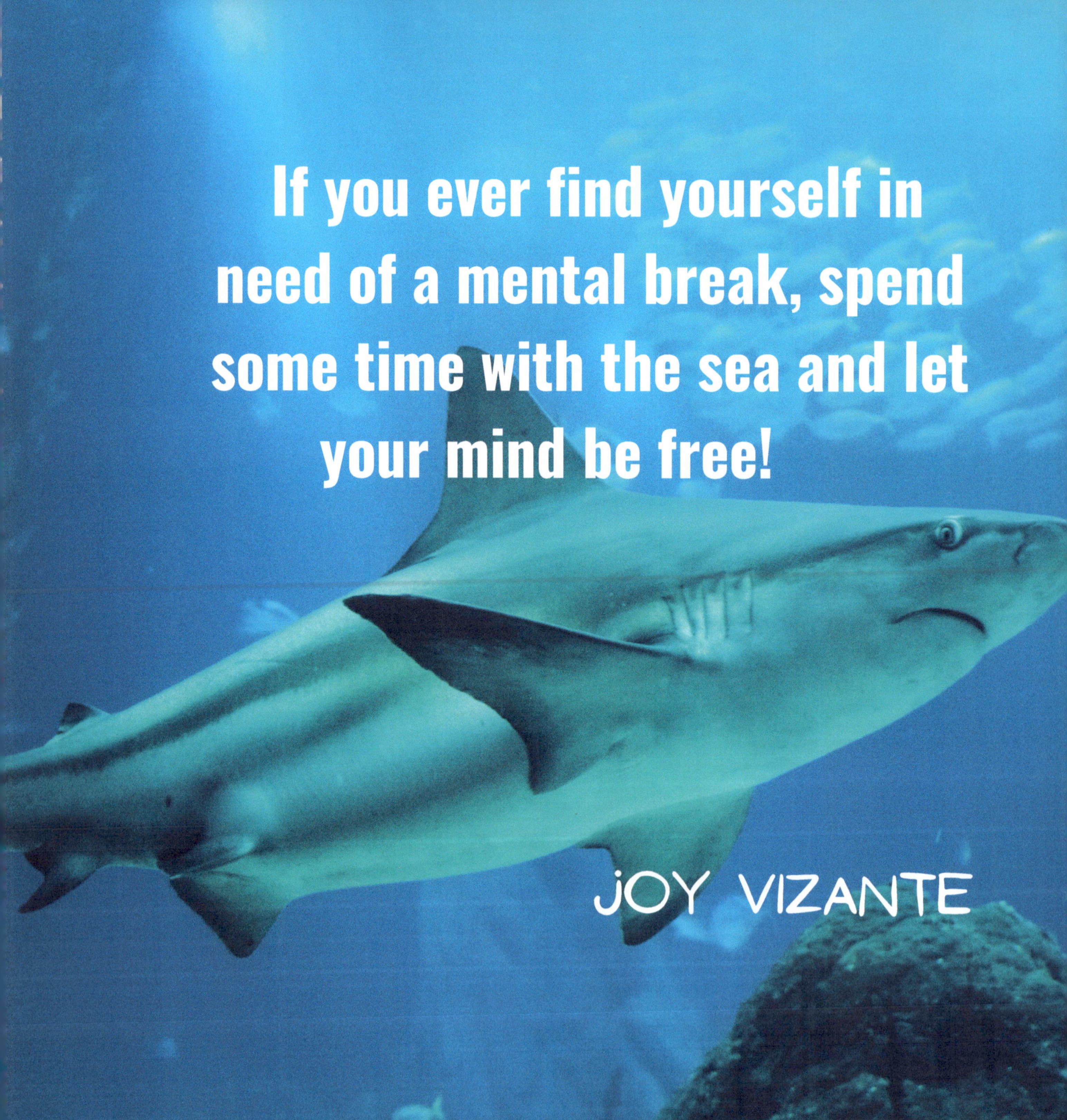

If you ever find yourself in need of a mental break, spend some time with the sea and let your mind be free!
JOY VIZANTE

MEET ME WHERE THE SKY
TOUCHES THE SEA!

Jennifer Donnelly

AT SEA, I LEARNED HOW
LITTLE A PERSON NEEDS, NOT
HOW MUCH.

Robin Lee Graham

THE SEA ALWAYS FILLED HER WITH LONGING, THOUGH FOR WHAT SHE WAS NEVER SURE.

Cornelia Funke

MY SOUL IS FULL OF LONGING FOR THE SECRET OF THE SEA, AND THE HEART OF THE GREAT OCEAN SENDS A THRILLING PULSE THROUGH ME.

Henry Wadsworth Longfellow

THE SEA IS AN
UNDERWATER MUSEUM
STILL AWAITING ITS
VISITORS.

Phillip Diole

LIVE IN THE SUNSHINE,
SWIM THE SEA, DRINK THE
WILD AIR.

Ralph Waldo Emerson

THE SEA, ONCE IT CASTS
ITS SPELL, HOLDS ONE IN
ITS NET OF WONDER
FOREVER.

Jacques Yves Cousteau

FOLLOW THE RIVER AND
YOU WILL FIND THE SEA.

French Proverb

I BELIEVE IN THE OCEAN
CURING ALL BAD MOODS.

Unknown

IF THE OCEAN CAN CALM ITSELF, SO CAN YOU. WE ARE BOTH SALT WATER MIXED WITH AIR

Nayyirah Waheed

DANCE WITH THE WAVES,
MOVE WITH THE SEA. LET
THE RHYTHM OF THE
WATER SET YOUR SOUL
FREE.

Christy Ann Martine

YOU CAN NEVER CROSS
THE OCEAN UNTIL YOU
HAVE COURAGE TO LOSE
SIGHT OF THE SHORE.

Christopher Columbus

WE DREAM IN COLORS
BORROWED FROM THE SEA.

Unknown

TAKE ME TO THE OCEAN.
LET ME SAIL THE OPEN SEA.
TO BREATHE THE WARM
AND SALTY AIR AND DREAM
OF THINGS TO BE.

Erica Billups

SMELL THE SEA AND FEEL
THE SKY. LET YOUR SOUL
AND SPIRIT FLY

Van Morrison

IN ONE DROP OF WATER
ARE FOUND ALL THE
SECRETS OF ALL THE
OCEANS.

Kahlil Gibran

WHY DO WE LOVE THE SEA?
IT IS BECAUSE IT HAS SOME
POTENT POWER TO MAKE
US THINK THINGS WE LIKE
TO THINK.

Robert Henri

THE CURE FOR ANYTHING IS
SALT WATER: SWEAT,
TEARS OR THE SEA.

Isak Dinesen